CONTENTS

Panch Thal
BRAC, Bangladesh (via Oxfam Trading)

See page 32

QUILTS FOR A FAIRER WORLD

First published in 1992
by Charles Letts & Co Ltd
Letts of London House
Parkgate Road
London SW11 4NQ

Created and produced by Rosemary Wilkinson
4 Lonsdale Square, London N1 1EN

Designer: Patrick Knowles
Photographers: Jerry Mullaney, Mark Gatehouse

ISBN 1 85238 352 6

A CIP catalogue record for this book is available
from the British Library

The quilts in this book are from the Oxfam
Anniversary Theme at Quilts U.K. The Oxfam
Anniversary co-ordinator of the event was
Rachel Edge. She would like to thank everyone
who supported the event: all those who entered
the quilts and all who came to view them.

Printed and bound in Spain

INTRODUCTION

It is a great pleasure to write this introduction, as it was to see the quilts, to judge them with my two colleagues, and to read the explanations and thoughts behind them.

It is especially appropriate for Oxfam and Quilts U.K. to be linked in this fiftieth anniversary year. Patchwork and quilting are crafts concerned with thrift and recycling. Oxfam shares these qualities. They are shown in the Oxfam shops where one person's cast-offs become another's treasured bargains. They are shown when Oxfam supporters use spare fabric or wool to make garments for children overseas - as depicted on two of the quilts in this book. Other quilts have been pieced, in the traditional way, with fabric salvaged from Oxfam shop clothing.

Oxfam also recycles in a far wider sense. People, who have previously been caught in a vicious cycle of deprivation, despair and disaster, can be given hope and the chance of sharing in sustainable development. This is the theme of many of the quilts here, and is demonstrated in concrete form by the quilts from overseas, brought to Quilts U.K. by Oxfam Trading.

Reading the quiltmakers' accounts has been a most moving experience. There is so great a diversity of interpretation, craftsmanship and care displayed - and this, in turn, illustrates the fact that it is not only "overseas" that Oxfam develops people. Thousands of Oxfam workers, paid and unpaid, have found that their lives have been enriched, and their talents developed by their experience of Oxfam. I know this is true for me, I am sure it is true for the makers of these quilts, and I hope it will be true for those who read and enjoy this book.

Gillian M. Clarke
Oxfam volunteer and trustee

Out of Darkness
Diana Brockway, Newport, Gwent

Freedom from want and bondage are symbolically suggested through a lifting up from darkness into light. The 'Mariner's Compass' patchwork centre is surrounded by Hawaiian appliqué. Around this is an inner frame of earth-coloured patches appliquéd with white flowers and a chain-link of unity. The knotted rope border reiterates the theme of togetherness passing through water and light to images of life-sustaining crops and world peace. Machine pieced, hand quilted, hand and machine appliqué.

FIRST PRIZE: OXFAM THEME

42 x 42 in (107 x 107 cm)

Levelling the Odds

Pam Ironmonger, Brixham, Devon

This quilt is charged with symbols to illustrate the many different aspects of Oxfam. The restricted colours and materials are self-imposed limitations to mirror the way the Third World works within its limits. The cloth is cheap, unbleached calico denoting the paucity of underdeveloped countries. The thread is a symbol of the work of Oxfam in its attempt to transform the situation and draw together the humanity of the developed countries. The face in the central panel is based on a playing card and represents the element of chance involved in the country of one's birth. Cord quilting, hand quilting, machine quilting.

FIRST PRIZE: THE MOST EXCITING USE OF THE SEWING MACHINE

42 x 50 in (107 x 127 cm)

Rags to Riches Oxfam 1942-1992

Kathy Morton, Sutton-in-Ashfield, Nottinghamshire

Last year Oxfam's 'Wastesaver' operation in Huddersfield processed £378,000 worth of rags and foil. This quilt also sets out to turn 'rags into riches'. The fabrics used were all purchased from the local Oxfam shop. Hand pieced and quilted.

SECOND PRIZE: OXFAM THEME

64 x 85 in (163 x 216 cm)

Live Simply

Anne-Marie Stewart, Ipswich, Suffolk

A blue sky surrounds the lace Oxfam symbol, which represents a fragile world. Wheat, potential food for the whole world, is more precious than metals, hence its copper colour. The triangles suggest a multi-ethnic dimension. Fabric painting, stencilling, dyeing, machine appliqué, piecing and quilting.

THIRD PRIZE: OXFAM THEME

SECOND PRIZE: FABRIC PAINTING (INDIVIDUAL)

37 x 47 in (94 x 119 cm)

Waste Not, Want Not

Catherine Williams, Bishop's Stortford, Essex

All the different items - household objects, books, clothing - that people donate to Oxfam shops are turned into cash by Oxfam to fund agricultural projects in poorer countries. Actual coins stuck onto the quilt come from various parts of the world. The quilt was made in appreciation of the charity that clothed the maker when she was broke and for her father, who has always supported Oxfam. Hand stitched throughout.

SECOND PRIZE: HUMOUR

32 x 35 in (81 x 89 cm)

February Leap Frogs
Surrey Young Quilters, Dorking, Surrey

On 29th February, 1992, Oxfam's nationwide fund raising day, a 'Stitch 'n' Stencil' day for young quilters was held in a shop in Epsom, Surrey. The day began at 10 a.m. and six quilters aged between seven and twelve years took part. The stencils - of Oxfam frogs and a leafy Oxfam design - were planned and cut by Penny Alder. Each person stencilled a frog and a leaf block plus an extra frog block to take home. Everyone then helped to machine stitch the blocks to the green sashing strips and to tie the quilt with embroidery floss. By 3 p.m. the quilt was finished and £19 had been raised for Oxfam during the day.

SECOND PRIZE: FABRIC PAINTING (GROUP)

37 x 47 in (94 x 119 cm)

Life's a Game
Kiran Williams (11 years old), Wolverhampton, Staffordshire

Read the instructions and play the game with a felt die and felt suns for counters. Oxfam is fighting for good; two dragons represent good and evil - the green for water, fertility, agriculture and the brown for drought, barren soils and hunger. The game is painted with fabric crayons and the border made by patchwork squares. Machine pieced and hand quilted.

SPECIAL AWARD

32 x 44 in (81 x 112 cm)

Recyclomat

Rita Ball, Callington, Cornwall

A playmat inspired by the Australian Wagga Wagga quilts. The garments used were all purchased from Oxfam and applied to a blanket - also from Oxfam. Hand appliqué, hand finishing.

SPECIAL AWARD

52 x 72 in (132 x 183 cm)

Need and Greed
Catherine Macleod, Frodsham, Cheshire

The central image was inspired by a photograph of a priest holding the hand of a starving Ugandan boy. It is superimposed over contrasting pictures of the Third World and the Developed World, set within the Oxfam globe logo. Machine appliqué, hand embroidery.

SPECIAL AWARD

42 x 42 in (107 x 107 cm)

Sew Many Mouths to Feed

Peartree Quilters, St. Albans, Hertfordshire

The Oxfam logo was the starting point and the central image of this quilt, then each group member chose to depict a child from a country where Oxfam works, not forgetting a British child representing Oxfam's work in the U.K. among the disadvantaged. The quilting shows ears of corn symbolizing food for the world. Hand and machine appliqué, machine strip piecing, hand quilting.

SECOND PRIZE: GROUP ENTRY OVER 16

62 x 78 in (158 x 198 cm)

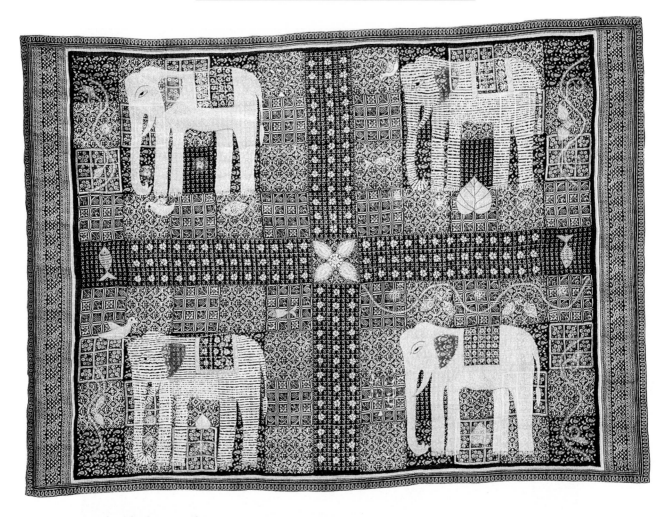

Kantha Elephant Quilt
Seva Sangh Samity & Panchannagram Mahila Samity, co-ordinated by Sasha, Calcutta,
India (via Oxfam Trading)

The quilt has a white block-printed design on a black silk ground. It was printed by
Brindaban Ghosh, and a Kantha-work design was added on top by a group called
Panchannagram Mahila Samity. Nakshi Kantha is a craft developed as a way of
recycling old cloth (especially saris and dhotis) in West Bengal and Bangladesh. The
pieces are quilted together with a running stitch closely worked all over the piece,
then coloured threads (perhaps from the border of a sari) are used to embroider the
designs on the 'new' cloth. Elephants are a very popular motif. Block-printed and
hand stitched.

SPECIAL AWARD

59 x 82 in (150 x 208 cm)

Maroon Block-printed Silk Quilt

Seva Sangh Samity & Self-help Handcrafts Society, co-ordinated by Sasha, Calcutta, India (via Oxfam Trading)

The quilt has a traditional Indian paisley design printed on silk. The design was developed by Sasha Exports of Calcutta, India. Brindaban Ghosh, a master printer, block-printed the cloth, and it was stitched by an association of textile workers. The quilting follows the paisley pattern. Block-printed and hand quilted.

59 x 83 in (150 x 211 cm)

Positively Fair

Philippa Johnston, Sutton, Surrey

The centre panel of this wallhanging represent harshness, sterility and the apparent hopelessness of nature and life. By contrast, the outer panels depict the possible fertility of nature and benefits to people's lives when they are given positive aid to help themselves. A combination of patchwork, appliqué, quilting and embroidery is used. All stitched by hand.

57 x 70 in (145 x 178 cm)

Meadows

Bristol Quilters Afternoon Group, Bristol

Made to demonstrate quilting-at-the-frame during an exhibition, this group quilt was designed by Barbara Duncan, whose husband designed and made the frame. The Afternoon Group does all its work for charity and all the fabrics for this piece were donated. It is a combination of two very simple blocks with colour interest added by the subtle shading from delicate to deep rich tones. Hand pieced and quilted.

66 x 90 in (168 x 229 cm)

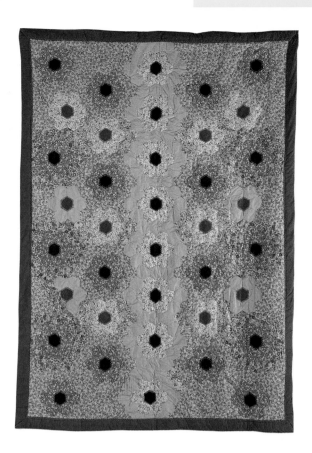

A Silk Purse
K. Tombs, Cobham, Surrey

Making use of available resources, this bed quilt is designed around a batch of patches donated to the Oxfam shop where the maker works. All had to be unpicked and the papers cut again with a new template - hence the title. It is made up of over 1,020 hexagons, all hand pieced, quilted in-the-ditch round the hexagon flowers and embroidered with feather stitching.

74 x 100 in (188 x 254 cm)

Over the Rainbow
Kate Williams (7 years, 10 months old), Wolverhampton, Staffordshire

A first quilt by a young quiltmaker to show her support for Oxfam. The rainbow image, painted with fabric crayons, was chosen because it is a mixture of good and bad mirroring Oxfam's achievements in combatting poverty and hunger. Machine pieced border and binding, hand quilted.

35 x 26 in (89 x 66 cm)

Round the World Bazaar

Avril Lansdell, Kingston-upon-Thames, Surrey

The six picture blocks on this cot quilt are appliquéd with hand-painted silk motifs taken from the 1990/91 Oxfam catalogue, showing a chicken, a lizard, a cat, a fish, a horse and an elephant. Extra details are embroidered. Fabric painting, hand and machine quilting, and hand appliqué and embroidery.

28 x 37 in (71 x 94 cm)

Golden Harvest

Hitchin Oxfam Shop Group, Hitchin, Hertfordshire

'Golden Harvest' shows how Oxfam during its fifty years of working for a fairer world has changed its cash donations to the Third World into practical self-help to alleviate hunger. It uses 75% recycled fabrics, with hand and machine-stitched patchwork and embroidery, finished with hand quilting.

48 x 64 in (122 x 163 cm)

Detail from Round the World Bazaar

Oxfam - Working for a Fairer World
Pauline Jackson, Broughton-in-Furness, Cumbria

An appliqué picture quilt inspired by Oxfam's work helping others to help themselves. In the foreground, the bridge, showing people joining together to help each other, passes over the all-essential water, which is accessible to all. The centre shows people at work cutting wood, tilling fields and planting crops, against a background of fruitful trees, green pastures and a bright sun to symbolize hope. The cottage in Oxford and the home in Africa link Oxfam and the workers. Embroidery, hand and machine appliqué and piecing.

72 x 90 in (183 x 229 cm)

Ragtime in Blue
Aeileish Watts, Worcester, Worcestershire

An Oxfam picture was the starting point for this wallhanging. No fabric was bought, only old clothes, of cuts and scraps were used after being dyed to give a uniform tonal quality. The loose strips on the border are like prayer flags (or hopes) and the maker would encourage other people to add their own strips. Patchwork and appliqué, all machine stitched.

34 x 53 in (86 x 135 cm)

You Can Help Too!
Hannah Watts (12 years old), Worcester, Worcestershire

A small wallhanging inspired by Oxfam's work and depicting the aspects which the maker thinks are the nicest: providing water and saving waste. The yellow background represents the sun over the world. All machine stitched.

18 x 24 in (46 x 61 cm)

Oxfam Star
Constance Sara, Stroud, Gloucestershire

Justice is at the heart of all aid and development issues both at home and abroad. Richer, stronger members of a family share with the poorer members not out of pity or charity but because it's fair. The heart of the block is therefore a modification of a block called 'Fair Play' (first published in 1922, see "Quilter's Album of Blocks and Borders", Jinny Beyer). The original is curved but the maker squared it because it seemed to symbolize justice better than the curve. We do speak of square deals and things being fair and square. This is set in the traditional 'Variable Star' because stars signify hope, striving, aspiration - and this much-used traditional pattern also acknowledges the maker's connection and debt to all the other quilters past and present to whom she is deeply grateful. A whole spectrum of colours is used to celebrate the fairer world and as a contrast to the characteristically monochrome images of poverty. Almost entirely hand pieced and machine quilted.

57 x 72 in (145 x 183 cm)

Oxfam Sampler
Averil Clavey, Cockermouth, Cumbria

A wallhanging inspired by Oxfam's work. The lettering and designs come from an Oxfam catalogue. Mirror work using milk bottle tops, postage stamps in the seminole patchwork and newspaper print fabric all symbolize the theme of recycling. Machine and hand pieced, machine quilted.

39 x 56 in (99 x 142 cm)

23

Round a Fairer World
Pam Le Bas, Leicester, Leicestershire

Symbolized human skin colours occupy roughly equal proportions of the background patchwork: in the real world, very unequal shares made the message still necessary on Oxfam's 50th anniversary. The Oxfam globe symbol is quilted in the corners of the patchwork. Machine pieced patchwork, hand appliqué and quilting.

58 x 69 in (147 x 175 cm)

Go for Grow
Janet Cook, Felmersham, Bedford

Dark, bare, brown worlds with Oxfam's help become green and gold with ripening crops. The stars are for the hope in the future, and the lack of borders and use of interlinking, interdependent patterns, based on the traditional block 'Variable Star', represent Oxfam's aims. Machine pieced, hand quilted, some hand dyeing.

30 x 36 in (76 x 92 cm)

Peace and Plenty
Danetre Quilters, Northampton

At the centre of this group quilt is the 'Tree of Life' surrounded by four golden triangles which signify Oxfam's Golden Jubilee. The quilted design in these triangles depicts Cornucopia, the horn of plenty. The sixteen blocks around the edge were chosen because their names are associated with Oxfam's work and ideals: 'Around the World'; 'Peace and Plenty'; 'Brave World'; 'Schoolhouse'; 'Bread Basket'; 'Windmill'; 'Friendship' and a 'Dove of Peace'. The quilting patterns used are a chain, symbolizing help and friendship, and the Oxfam logo which looks like a flower. The earth colours of yellow and brown at the bottom, move to greens for crops and new growth, then to blues at the top to represent sky and water. The quilt is made of cotton and polycotton fabrics, and was hand pieced and hand quilted.

55 x 56 in (140 x 142 cm)

Finished is Better than Perfect
Mary Slade, Kings Norton, Birmingham

A wallhanging made under pressure of time between family and work duties. The design is based on the concept of interlocking worlds, such as the 'Third World' and the 'New World', and the way they affect one another. Strong, bright and dark colours, often Amish-type shades are used. Hand and machine pieced and quilted.

40 x 40 in (102 x 102 cm)

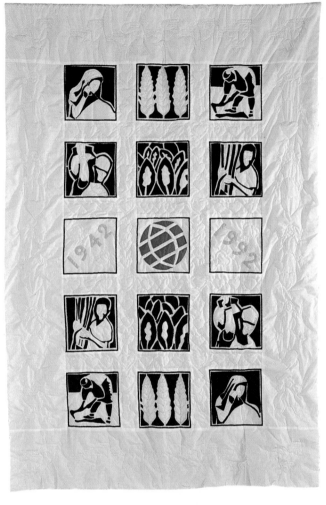

Depicting Oxfam
Ilford Oxfam Group, Ilford, Essex

From a group of workers in an Oxfam shop, this wallhanging is a pictorial record of the aims and initiatives of Oxfam. Brightly-coloured pieces against a strong background are hand applied and embroidered.

46 x 67 in (117 x 170 cm)

Oxfam in Action
Oxfam Shop Group, Newcastle-under-Lyme, Staffordshire

Inspired by Oxfam publicity material and showing Oxfam in action in the Third World. The quilted animals are taken from designs on ancient Inca fabrics, similar to those on current South American crafts sold in Oxfam shops. The quilt was made by a group of twelve workers in an Oxfam shop and the heart quilting patterns shows that it was sewn with love. Hand appliqué and quilting.

63 x 94 in (160 x 239 cm)

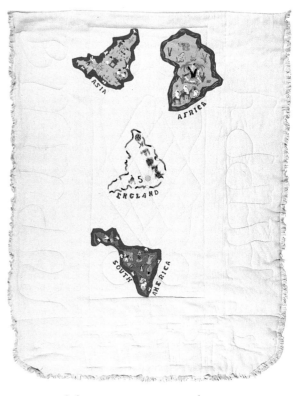

Star of Hope
Maureen Hoyle, Lymm, Cheshire

A miniature bed quilt made into a pattern the maker has called 'Star of Hope', using 3/8 in (9 mm) hexagons in blue, tan and pale peach. Hand pieced over papers, tie quilted with French knots.

15 x 17 in (38 x 43 cm)

Happy Birthday
Fedanp, Colombia (via Oxfam Trading)

The quilt has pictorial maps of the three main continents in which Oxfam works, around a map of England where the charity is based. Hand appliqué and embroidery, machine assembled.

89 x 114 in (226 x 290 cm)

Detail from Star of Hope (above)

Oxfam - A Friend to the World
Mary Mayne, Dunstable, Bedfordshire

A special tribute to a worthy cause. The world fabric is made up of tiny scraps of material trapped under a layer of organza. The green base fabrics and the yellow and orange sun rays at the top are shaded with transfer dyes. The border is made of folded triangles using a Thai technique. Hand dyed and quilted, machine pieced and appliquéd.

50 x 57 in (127 x 145 cm)

Trip Round the World
Dorothy Organ, Epping, Essex

This wallhanging is based on the design 'Trip Around the World' and is pieced in Oxfam's colours: blue and yellow. The blankets, tents, seeds and water (equipment) that Oxfam give are incorporated into the design. All the fabric was taken from the rag bag at the local Oxfam shop. Even the cotton was found in a bag of mixed items. The only new things were the 2 oz wadding and the needles. Machine pieced, hand quilted.

62 x 78 in (158 x 198 cm)

A Helping Hand, A Loving Heart
Rosemary Southam, Chalfont St. Peter, Buckinghamshire

With inspiration from the colourful batik and other ethnic textiles in the Oxfam catalogue, ideas from 'Traditional Quiltworks' and 'Piecemakers' calendar and encouragement from family and quilting friends, the quilt just grew. Hand and machine appliqué, machine pieced and quilted. Hand embroidered.

48 x 53 in (122 x 135 cm)

Together in Harmony
Margaret Smith, Shipton Oliffe, Cheltenham, Gloucestershire

This single bed quilt has been made for the maker's son. The design is a variation of 'Roman Stripe' and the colours chosen symbolize the red blood that binds us all, black and white together. Black in-the-ditch quilting shows a distinct pattern on the red backing fabric. Hand and machine pieced, hand quilted.

65 x 85 in (165 x 216 cm)

Tree of Life
Elizabeth Skinner, West Haddon, Northamptonshire

This is the tree of life that Oxfam strives to sustain, flanked by blood-red hearts of love, edged by water and sun, also essential to our existence. Hand pieced, quilted and beaded.

34 x 34 in (86 x 86 cm)

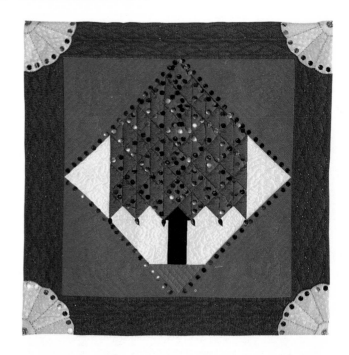

The Golden Future
Boxgrove and Merrow Townswomen's Guild, Guildford, Surrey

The brown and blue squares have an appliquéd Oxfam globe symbol and ears of wheat to illustrate world food aid. The blue border rectangles with their branch motifs denote tree planting overseas and the brown corner squares have gold ingots (for the 50 years) illustrating the countries receiving aid. Hand sewing, machine appliqué and embroidery.

45 x 67 in (114 x 170 cm)

One World to Share

Mary Stevens, Southam, Warwickshire

Verdant motifs flow around the world set against a cream background. The images show birds and beasts, tractors for our shared technologies and figures representing our talents. The borders are quilted with designs from the Oxfam catalogue and quilted corner motifs depict the bread (wheat) and fishes from the Bible story of the feeding of the five thousand. Hand appliqué and quilting.

45 x 45 in (114 x 114 cm)

Sewn for Oxfam

Norine Redman, Milton Keynes, Buckinghamshire

A bed quilt inspired by the pattern on Oxfam bags and made entirely with fabrics donated by friends in Portsmouth and Milton Keynes. The lettering is made from hand-made bias binding, the clothes are machine stitched and outline quilted by hand. The bird pattern is also hand-quilted.

47 x 76 in (119 x 193 cm)

Panch Thal

BRAC, Bangladesh (via Oxfam Trading)

Fish motifs, a variety of animals and people, together with a mango pattern, make up this Nakshi Kantha worked bedspread. This style of quilting is traditional to Bangladesh (see page 16). Hand stitched.

67 x 98 (170 x 249 cm)

Everlasting Spring
Grupo Asociativo Los Andes, Colombia (via Oxfam Trading)

The quilt was designed by Flor Alba Paz, a member of the Los Andes Cooperative. She describes the quilt as follows: 'There is not a story behind the title, but rather a message. We should admire nature and help to preserve it, and keep our flora and fauna so we'll always have plenty of both. In this way, Nature will always be a present reality, instead of part of our history'. Machine appliqué, hand embroidered, machine assembled.

31 x 66 in (79 x 167 cm)

Ethnic (above)
Margaret Hughes, Anglesey, Gwynedd

'Ethnic' is intended as a bold statement of the Oxfam Anniversary, designed as a backdrop for a small Oxfam shop window. Felt and sacking fabrics and colours are 'earthy' to emphasize the simplicity. The Oxfam logo is used as an eye-catcher. Appliqué, quilting and embroidery by hand, machine assembly.

40 x 23 in (102 x 59 cm)

Children of the World
Four Oaks First School, Sutton Coldfield, West Midlands

Every child in the school had a part in making this single bed quilt. The figures drawn on the border show children from all over the world, which is represented by the globe appliquéd in the centre. The Oxfam 'leap frog' and the numbers celebrate the fifty years of working for a fairer world. Fabric crayon painting, hand embroidery, hand and machine stitching.

48 x 78 in (122 x 198 cm)

33

The Catherine Quilt
Catherine Infant School Friday Sewing Group,
Leicester, Leicestershire

The idea for the quilt came from hearing about the American 'quilting bees', where a group of people meet to make a collaborative quilt. The design of this small wallhanging represents threads of lives coming together to form the basis of one world of shared beliefs, cultures, peace and equality. The execution of the techniques reflects the ethnic cultures of the twelve, six-year-old children who worked on the quilt. Batik and hand painting, embroidery, hand quilting and machine piecing.

31 x 35 in (78 x 89 cm)

To a Fairer World
Maggie Ward, Grandpont, Oxford

Inspired by a London Underground poster "To Fresh Air" by Maxwell Armfield (1915). The circular Oxfam Anniversary world logo replaces one of the circles, which coincidentally was green and white on the original poster. Machine appliqué.

20 x 28 in (51 x 71 cm)

Fruits of the Earth for All
Launton Ladies Sewing Circle, Bicester, Oxfordshire

A group quilt made entirely from donated fabrics. Within a frame of fruits and leaves of the vine, the design depicts never-ending, earth brown paths circulating golden grain to all corners of the world past flashes of bright flowers and blue sky. Hand stitched patchwork, appliqué and quilting.

43 x 35 in (109 x 89 cm)

Working Together
Margot Agnew, Chorley, Lancashire

A large wallhanging inspired by the late Dorothy Bassett, an Oxfam worker from 1970 to 1985; Secretary of the Chorley Oxfam Group and member of the Oxfam Central Council of Management from 1978 to 1980. The images of women watering crops and hoeing the soil are taken from Oxfam leaflets. Couched threads represent the water and raffia the crops. Machine appliqué, hand and machine embroidery.

142 x 96 in (361 x 244 cm)

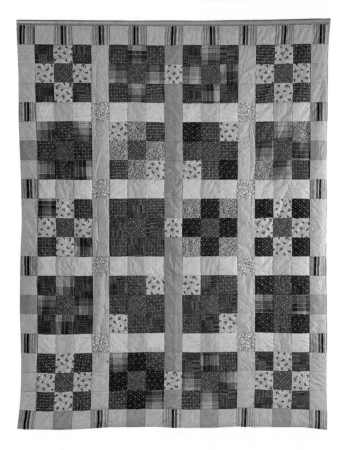

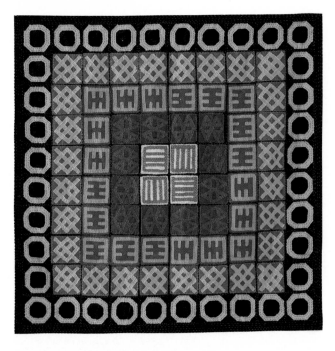

Oxfam Kaleidoscope

Pam Keeling, Barton Seagrave, Kettering, Northamptonshire

The block patterns for this wallhanging are the result of a 'doodle' made during a conference when thinking about the competition. The raw-edged pieces are applied by hand with a running stitch and hand pieced.

45 x 45 in (114 x 114 cm)

Pink Medley

Didcot Townswomen's Guild, Didcot, Oxfordshire

The choice of colours was based on the various shades of pink in a cottage garden, and the design was inspired by illustrations in an old book of nursery rhymes. Hand pieced throughout.

66 x 84 in (168 x 213 cm)

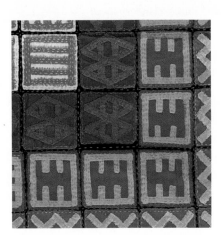

Detail from Oxfam Kaleidoscope

Knit One for Me

Portishead Quilters, Portishead, Bristol

A celebration of the Oxfam knitted vest and the first competition quilt by this group. Twenty members were each given pieces of unbleached calico, a knitting pattern and a body template; there were no rules about how they should be put together. The result: fifty completely different Oxfam vests and models with all kinds of extras, such as beads, baskets and little hats. Hand knitting, appliqué, and quilting, machine piecing.

75 x 150 in (191 x 381 cm)

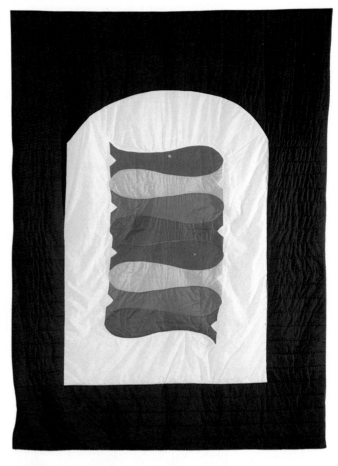

Oxfam - Working for a Fairer World
Kathy Morton, Sutton-in-Ashfield, Nottinghamshire

A wallhanging featuring an explosion of colours and shapes in celebration of the tireless commitment of tens of thousands of volunteers 'working for a fairer world'. Hand stitched patchwork and quilting.

65 x 94 in (165 x 239 cm)

Food from the Sea
Tric Watkins, Trescott, Wolverhampton

The design of this wallhanging was inspired by a photograph printed in an Oxfam catalogue of a woven rug from Salasaca, the main weaving centre of Ecuador. The fish are in the colours of Maltese fishing boats and the brown border has the effect of a window frame. Hand piecing, quilting and appliqué.

76 x 96 in (193 x 244 cm)

Launceston Helps Too!

Launceston Oxfam Helpers, Cornwall

A wallhanging with a central, strip-pieced mandala showing ten figures holding hands around the Oxfam globe logo, surrounded by decorative panels showing the local Oxfam shop and other landmarks of the area. The motto and the borders are appliquéd with doves and leaves of peace. Hand quilting, appliqué and embroidery; machine stitching.

46 x 57 in (117 x 145 cm)

Oxflag

Year 8, Chauncy School, Ware, Hertfordshire

Flags were the most popular of the ideas which children in this class of twelve to thirteen-year-olds produced for the quilt, so the flag design was chosen to make a wallhanging. It is also a simple shape for a first piece of machine stitching. Twenty different flags are shown together with a centrepiece of the globe. Machine appliqué, hand quilting.

47 x 70 in (119 x 178 cm)

Celebration
Jane Wheat, Radcliffe-on-Trent, Nottinghamshire

A design arising out of a collection made over many years of people from all over the world. From a colour photocopy the images were transfer printed onto fabrics and each portrait is given equal space on the quilt to represent a fairer world in which all races have an equal value. The blue and green colours of the patchwork symbolize water and fertility and the whole is a celebration of the work of Oxfam. Machine piecing, hand quilting and appliqué.

45 x 45 in (114 x 114 cm)

Light Up the World
Mary Hewson, New Milton, Hampshire

Cottons and silks from Indonesia, India, Africa, Japan, Thailand, Europe and America, representing as many rich and poor nations as possible, are used to illustrate the Oxfam logo as a world spinning through space. Machine pieced, embroidered and quilted.

30 x 20 in (76 x 51 cm)

Happy Smiling Faces
Jenny Morgan, Llandrindod Wells, Powys

A wallhanging, from an original design by Judy Martin, showing children of all nations linking arms across their different backgrounds. Machine piecing, appliqué and quilting.

44 x 42 in (112 x 107 cm)

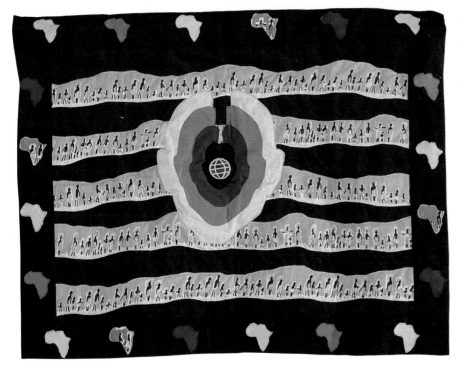

Many Miles
Jane Wheat, Radcliffe-on-Trent, Nottinghamshire

Oxfam's work has helped many people: the images of faces in the central appliqué and of marching figures in the strips of fabric from a recycled skirt and top are symbolic of this. Machine appliqué, hand and machine quilting.

35 x 27 in (89 x 69 cm)

From Rags to Riches
Beverley Wood, Winchester, Hampshire

A small wallhanging inspired by Oxfam's success in creating a fairer world by turning rags into funds which go directly to the Third World. The gold central globe is surrounded by borders worked in colours and patterns representing the many countries which Oxfam continues to support. Machine piecing, hand quilting and appliqué.

27 x 36 in (69 x 91 cm)

A Celebration in Colour
Hilda Bradbury, Bridgenorth, Shropshire

Inspired by the Oxfam trading catalogue, this is an interpretation of the vibrant colours and exciting design of goods produced by countries working for a fairer world. The silver motifs and the mirror work are Indian and the border has couched threads. Machine and hand pieced and embroidered, hand appliqué and quilting.

28 x 42 in (71 x 107 cm)

The Price of Freedom
Bernadette Falvey, Barna, Galway, Eire

The struggle against oppression is illustrated as a central wheel of minutely-pieced silk scraps exploding into frayed and shredded fragments, some trapped behind a layer of crystal organza. Machine pieced and quilted.

41 x 43 in (104 x 109 cm)

A Bit Like Snakes and Ladders
Sheila Arthurs, Castle Vale, Birmingham

Reading about the ups and downs of Oxfam's first 50 years reminded the maker of the children's games of 'Snakes and Ladders'. This idea was the starting point for a game quilt using as many colours as possible and with a fabric die and Oxfam globes for counters. Fabric painting, machine pieced, hand quilted.

55 x 55 in (140 x 140 cm)

Symbols of Hope
Measham Quilters, Swadlincote, Derbyshire

Produced by a beginners group experimenting with technique and colour, this wallhanging contains images of Oxfam and its work. The title represents positive work towards a fairer world. Appliqué, hand and machine quilting, embroidery, tie dyeing and fabric pen painting, strip patchwork.

37 x 37 in (94 x 94 cm)

Mali '85

Angela Raby, Northfield, Birmingham

The starting point for this wallhanging was a photograph of Mali taken in 1985 by Sebastião Salgado, an outstanding photographer. The image and the caption – 'Women and children wander the dried-out bed of a great lake. Their men have left to look for work. No money comes back' seem to epitomize the problems Oxfam faces. The words, in black for despair and yellow for hope, are to be read at a distance but seen as a pattern close up. The fabrics are recycled and types mixed to give textural interest: with orange velvet from some curtains, black from an old swimsuit and silks from a dressmaker. Hand piecing and appliqué, machine quilting and embroidery.

45 x 38 in (114 x 97 cm)

Colour Their World

Goblin Coombe Quilters, Cleeve, Avon

This group wallhanging depicts grey and black figures representing those people yet to be helped above brightly-coloured people who have had their lives enriched by Oxfam projects. As a border around them all, the chain design illustrates continuing aid. Machine and hand appliqué and embroidery, hand piecing and quilting.

59 x 45 in (150 x 114 cm)

The Oxfam Tree

Totternhoe Quilters, Dunstable, Bedfordshire

A piece of Nigerian fabric stored since the 1930s was the inspiration for this wallhanging. It is combined with other donated fabrics to make the central tree of life. Hung around this are twenty-five objects as symbols of Oxfam's worldwide work on the one side and its trading products on the other. The stencilled letters represent crate markings. Machine pieced, hand quilted.

45 x 45 in (114 x 114 cm)

Homeless
Rita Hodges, Berkhamsted, Hertfordshire

Homelessness as illustrated in this scene embodies the message 'Love your neighbour', which is the underlying theme of Oxfam's mission to work for a fairer world. The Amish colours are a reminder of the fact that they were once refugees and a symbol of the idea that yesterday's refugees are often tomorrow's quilters. Machine appliqué and quilting.

29 x 36 in (74 x 91 cm)

Communication
Maureen Cassells, Renfrew, Scotland

An optical illusion in bright, solid colours representing faces of people from many nations talking *and* listening. The inspiration being the importance of communication to ensure the best utilization of financial and practical assistance. Hand appliqué with hand and machine quilting.

48 x 48 in (122 x 122 cm)

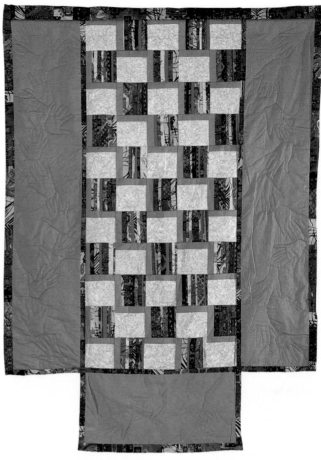

Earth, Sea and Sky

Avril Hopcraft, Milton Keynes, Buckinghamshire

An abstract interpretation of how Oxfam has helped thousands of people to appreciate the world in which they live. The quilting is stitched in a variety of different colours reflecting the flags of the countries which Oxfam helps. The cotton fabrics are all hand-dyed. Hand pieced and quilted.

52 x 48 in (132 x 122 cm)

Hands Across the Sands

Borderers Quilting Group, Ludlow, Shropshire

The inspiration for the quilt was thinking about the different nationalities of the world, their conflicts and problems. The hands depict the sharing and caring needed by so many. The ethnic designs on the fabric seemed right to represent a multi-cultural world. Machine pieced and hand quilted.

69 x 94 in (175 x 239 cm)

Detail from Earth, Sea and Sky (above)

United World
Maxine Addison, Whickham, Newcastle-on-Tyne

Three traditional blocks - 'Old World', 'New World' and 'Third World' are combined to produce this bed quilt. The message is spelt out in the square patches and the flowery patches beneath the message are symbolic of what the world can produce when we are united. Machine pieced.

82 x 95 in (208 x 241 cm)

Baskets of Love for a Fairer World
White Wells Quilters, Ilkley, West Yorkshire

A group quilt of red patterned baskets on black with red, gold and black hand printed and painted calico sashing. This quilt was made as part of Oxfam's Leap Day Appeal, as members gave up their day on 29th February, 1992, to work with love for a fairer world by making the blocks and sashing for the quilt top. Hand and machine appliqué and piecing, hand tied and quilted, hand printed and painted calico.

52 x 85 in (132 x 216 cm)

Detail from Baskets of Love for a Fairer World (left)

51

A Fairer Use of Those Practice Blocks
Berkhamstead Quilters, Bovingdon, Hertfordshire

The group wanted to take up the Oxfam quilt challenge, so the members pooled their collection of blocks and pieced them together. Various traditional patchwork patterns are included, such as 'Tumbling Blocks', 'Log Cabin', 'Nine Patch' and 'Wild Geese', with crazy patchwork and appliquéd blocks. The piece is hand quilted by the group with a sun and its rays radiating out to the Oxfam logos in the corners. Hand and machine piecing and appliqué, hand quilting.

53 x 67 in (135 x 170 cm)

From Oxfam to Oxfam
Irene Maxwell, Sidcup, Kent

The patterned material was purchased from an Oxfam shop to make this cot quilt for Oxfam: hence the title. The figures and letters are all Kantha work (see page 16) and the green background symbolizes hope for a green world. Hand stitched throughout.

32 x 37 in (81 x 94 cm)

Collector's Piece
Yvonne Blatchford, Shirley,
Southampton

A wallhanging depicting the
channelling of funds through
Oxfam into projects to help the
needy of the world. Transfer
paints have been used for the
bank notes and the other images
have been machine applied or
embroidered. Finished with
machine quilting.

39 x 29 in (99 x 74 cm)]

Our Fair World
Avonbourne School Quilters,
Bournemouth

A quilt made by a group of
eleven to sixteen-year-olds as an
after-school activity. All the
fabrics, apart from the hessian,
are recycled. Various dyeing
and printing techniques have
been used, combined with
different kinds of needlework to
fill the quilt with images of
Oxfam's work, from agriculture
and fishing to healthcare and
education. Ten different
templates of people make up the
central group where funds from
one group provide food for
another. Hand and machine
appliqué, strip patchwork,
embroidery, hand and machine
pieced, tie dyed and fabric
transfer painted

55 in (140 cm) diameter

Happy Homes

Orleton School, Orleton, Ludlow, Shropshire

This is the third quilt made by a group of eight to eleven-year-old children at the school. After a discussion about the work of Oxfam, it was decided to make patchwork houses using a variety of fabrics. It was great fun to make. Machine pieced and hand quilted.

48 x 48 in (122 x 122 cm)

Fernando the Cat

Sylvia Williams, Llandrindod Wells, Powys

A small wallhanging or cot quilt using an enlarged design and the colours from the maker's favourite Oxfam tea towel. The border is quilted with the Oxfam globe symbol. Machine piecing and appliqué, hand quilting and embroidery.

36 x 43 in (92 x 109 cm)

Time Well Spent

Yvonne Loudon, Portishead, Bristol

The colours of the 'world' progress from black to yellow and the block shapes change with the colours: the whole symbolizing the journey from darkness to light, from discord to harmony - our wish for a fairer world. Quilting in the borders reiterates this theme. All hand stitched.

50 x 72 in (127 x 183 cm)

55

Sewing Seeds

Sue Barry, Jenni Dobson, Mary Logan, Loughborough, Leicestershire

Open hand prints made by children around the edge and adults in the centre represent the give and take between international communities. The appliquéd seeds and the knotted ties (by children) representing plants symbolize Oxfam's contribution to self-help and consequent self-respect. Transfer dyed, machine assembled, hand appliqué, tie quilted.

59 x 60 in (150 x 152 cm)

Kendal Oxfam Fairer World Quilt

Kendal Oxfam Group, Kendal, Cumbria

The colour scheme of this bed quilt is inspired by the variety of skin colourings of the people for whom Oxfam works throughout the world. All the fabric is donated, so the theme developed loosely as suitable materials came to hand in the Oxfam shop. The message around the border is worked in chain stitch. Hand pieced and hand embroidered.

81 x 100 in (206 x 254 cm)

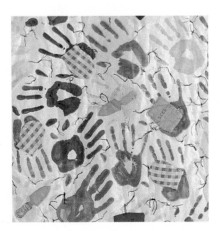

Detail from Sewing Seeds (above)

Bits and Pieces
Freda Lee, Windermere, Cumbria

This multi-colour, chevron style quilt was made by an Oxfam worker from lots of little pieces left over from other projects. It was made to show that anyone's surplus items can be used by Oxfam to work for a fairer world. The pieces are quilted in-the-ditch. Machine pieced, hand quilted.

81 x 87 in (206 x 221 cm)

Leaping for Oxfam
Lleyn Delyn Quilters, Mold, Clwyd

Over eighty quilters participated in this gift to Oxfam. Everyone volunteered (it's difficult to sew with your arm twisted behind your back!). The Oxfam leap frog has been appliquéd in the centre of the quilt, surrounded by other frog appliqués set amongst Nine Patch blocks. Hand and machine pieced, machine appliqué and quilting.

60 x 96 in (152 x 244 cm)

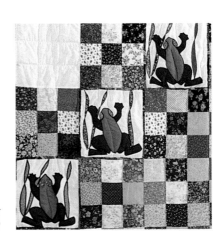

*Detail from Leaping
for Oxfam (left)*

Leaping for Life
Susan Hill, Wrexham, Clwyd

Many of the fabrics in this wallhanging were donated by friends. The patchwork frogs and fish are pictured in a blue pond surrounded by green plants. The inspiration behind the quilt was a combination of hearing about the Oxfam Leap Day Challenge and seeing a book on frogs and flowers on the same day. Hand stitched throughout.

60 x 50 in (152 x 127 cm)

For Oxfam with Love
Sheila Scawen, Bradwell, Sheffield

This wallhanging was started on Leap Day (29th February, 1992) in celebration of Oxfam's love and care for the peoples of the world. Machine pieced, hand appliqué and quilting.

37 x 40 in (94 x 102 cm)

Women of Hope
Sue Barry, Loughborough,
Leicestershire

The inspiration for this quilt
came from the undervaluing of
the work of women. Here
women are portrayed as hope
for the future. The earthy
colours represent their affinity
with the earth and the needs of
survival. Hand and machine
quilting, machine appliqué,
fabric painting and trapunto.

26 x 22 in (66 x 56 cm)

Fancy! One World
Jane Williams, Wolverhampton,
Staffordshire

The world within a star is
bordered by quilted Oxfam
symbols, the anniversary dates
and doves of peace. This
combination of ideas about
Oxfam is a first try for a
competition. Machine pieced,
hand appliqué and quilting.

48 x 48 in (122 x 122 cm)

The Oxfamily Tree
Jean England, Pury End, Northamptonshire

The crazy patchwork of the side panels represents the thousands of garments donated to Oxfam shops, also suggested by the coathangers embroidered at the top of the quilt. Anything that cannot be sold is parcelled up and sent for recycling; wool, for example, is made into blankets which are warehoused until needed (hence the little 3D wastesaver bags at the bottom). The tree shows the cycle of giving, producing and opportunities for self-help overseas. Hand patchwork, quilting and appliqué.

45 x 65 in (114 x 165 cm)

Worldwide

Raya Quilters, Tavistock, Devon

A graphic interpretation of Oxfam's worldwide work. The bands of fabric illustrate the cool, temperate and tropical regions of the earth surrounded by the deep blue of the oceans. The Oxfam globe is cut from one piece of fabric and appliquéd on top. The message is that Oxfam is working everywhere for a fairer world. Machine pieced, hand appliqué and quilting.

53 x 52 in (135 x 132 cm)

Oxfam

Joanne Pate, Keighley, Yorkshire

A two-sided quilt showing an interpretation of the fairer world theme in which all children are loved equally. The front of the quilt has the global message, the reverse shows the local efforts made by workers and customers in an Oxfam shop. Hand patchwork and appliqué, machine quilted.

61 x 70 in (155 x 178 cm)

It's in the Name
Dawn Berry, Cheltenham,
Gloucestershire

The four individual, traditional patchwork blocks which make up this hanging have been chosen for their titles. At the top is 'Our Village Green' for the people and communities that help and are helped. At the bottom 'Broken Dishes' suggests the disasters - both natural and man-made - for which assistance is so important. On the right side 'Corn and Beans' symbolizes the aid which is given and on the left 'Sunbeam' stands for the hope that Oxfam brings to those it helps. Almost all the materials used are left over from other projects. Hand pieced, tie quilted and plaited.

37 x 37 in (94 x 94 cm)

Oxfam
J. Scothern, Mapperley, Nottingham

A cot quilt using cotton fabrics in ten different colours. All the letters, numbers and images are embroidered in chain stitch to spell out the message. Hand and machine stitched.

29 x 32 in (74 x 81 cm)

Firework Celebration
Rosie Wood, Eastbourne, East Sussex

The black background of this wallhanging is stitched with multi-coloured embroidery to represent a burst of fireworks celebrating fifty years of Oxfam working for a fairer world. Beads, sequins and a ribbon border all add to the display for a golden anniversary. Machine stitched and embroidered.

23 x 45 in (58 x 114 cm)

Sea Harvest
Rosemary Gregory, Wolverhampton, Staffordshire

Inspired by a Kaffe Fassett tapestry, the design of this wallhanging reflects the tree planting and seawood farming industries in Indonesia. The yellows, oranges and browns depict the land; the green denotes the trees and the seawood. Machine patchwork and appliqué, hand quilting.

32 x 44 in (81 x 112 cm)

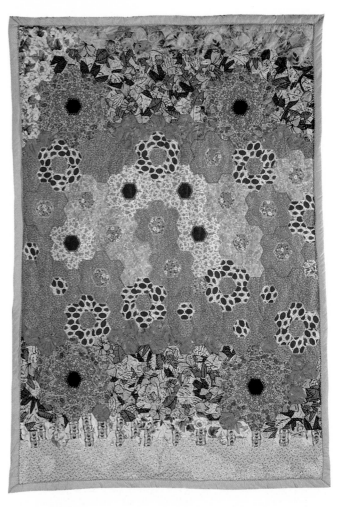

The Water Carriers

Maureen Evans, Southampton, Hampshire

This picture quilt was made entirely from donated fabrics. The two African women remind us that in the Western World we take clean running water for granted. Oxfam is helping others to set up their own water schemes for a fairer world. Hand appliqué, fabric painting, machine pieced border.

33 x 37 in (84 x 94 cm)

Necessity Is -

K. Tombs, Cobham, Surrey

All the fabrics in this quilt were offcuts from other projects, some left over from making shifts and shorts for children in the Third World: hence the random design of hexagons highlighted with feather stitching. Hand stitched throughout.

66 x 97 in (168 x 246 cm)

Detail from Four Corners (opposite)

Four Corners
Sara Greenwood, London

Made entirely from offcuts and recycled fabrics from many different countries, this bed quilt has as its starting point and central image the traditional patchwork block 'Trip Around the World'. Other ideas are displayed visually in the fabrics themselves or symbolically in the classic quilting patterns, such as 'Next Door Neighbours', 'Birds in the Air' and 'Friendship Star' and in the quilted designs such as the four trees chosen for their specific meanings in the Victorian language of flowers. There are grapes for charity, a flowering almond for hope, a juniper for succour and protection and a mistletoe for overcoming difficulties. Machine pieced, hand finished and quilted.

90 x 90 in (229 x 229 cm)

Padmasree Black
BRAC, Bangladesh (via Oxfam Trading)

A black Nakshi Kantha work bedspread with traditional motifs celebrating the links between people and nature. This style of quilting is worked by groups of women in villages all over Bangladesh (see page 16).

86 x 112 in (218 x 285 cm)

Fan Quilt - Raising the Wind for Oxfam
Dora Ryder, Kidderminster, Worcestershire

Multi-coloured fans are appliquéd with very light padding onto a Cambridge blue background. The fans are decorated with tatting and divided by feather stitching. Navy blue sashing strips, bordered by striped and 'Jacobean' fabrics set off the design. Machine pieced, handmade tatting, and hand embroidered.

*Detail from
Padmasree Black
(above)*

Reach Out
Geraldine Mundy, Milton Keynes, Buckinghamshire

This is a first quilt, made with gradation dyed fabrics in eight shades of green and hand quilted with a ripple effect to denote people reaching out to each other. Hand pieced over papers, hand quilted.

20 x 20 in (51 x 51 cm)

Oxfam: 50 Years Working for a Fairer World
YWCA Dhaka, Bangladesh (via Oxfam Trading)

Taking the shape of the Oxfam logo, the hanging has motifs taken from products in the Oxfam Trading catalogue, representing the countries with which Oxfam works. Appliqué work and embroidery on a hessian background. Hand stitched.

32 x 51 in (81 x 130 cm)

Detail from Oxfam: 50 Years Working for a Fairer World (left)

67

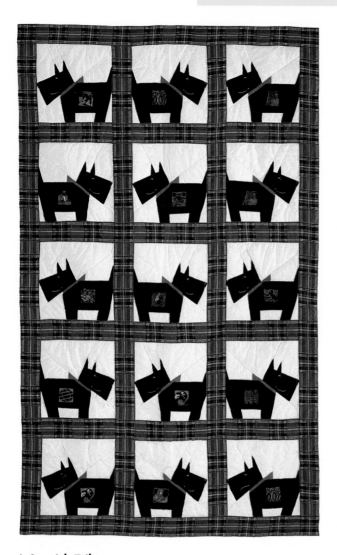

A Scottish Tribute

Bothwell Quilters, Glasgow, Scotland

Fifteen black Scottie dogs each displaying an image from the Oxfam catalogue, set into a cream background and assembled with sashing strips in Royal Stuart tartan, present a tribute from Scotland to the work of Oxfam. Hand pieced and quilted.

51 x 80 in (130 x 203 cm)

Reverse Appliqué Bed Quilt

Sabina Co-op, Ahmedabad, India (via Oxfam Trading)

A bed quilt with a rich green and pink design created with reverse appliqué, on a cream ground. This technique for using up scraps (known as chindi) from the textile mills of Ahmedabad, is typical of the area. Sabina is a cooperative of women who work with this chindi. Little mirrors are sewn at the intersections of the blocks. Hand stitched.

57 x 88 in (145 x 224 cm)

Celebrating Oxfam's Anniversary
Taller Libertad, Colombia (via Oxfam Trading)

A scene of celebration with children playing games and swimming, people working in fields full of crops and a sky full of the sun, birds, clouds and a rainbow. Hand appliqué and embroidery, machine assembled.

89 x 114 in (226 x 290 cm)

Animals with Flower Border
BRAC, Bangladesh (via Oxfam Trading)

A bedspread with traditional motifs - fish, suns, animals and people - worked in springtime colours of green, blue and gold. This is Nakshi Kantha work, a traditional style of quilting from Bangladesh (see page 16). Hand stitched.

79 x 90 in (200 x 229 cm)

Help Them Make the Desert Flower
Lynn Cooke, Malvern, Worcestershire

This wallhanging was inspired by words spoken by M. Buerk, a BBC reporter, during the appeal for funds for Ethiopia. He described what he saw there in the following words: "Dawn, and as the sun breaks through the piercing chill of night it lights a Biblical famine". Superimposed on an interpretation of this image are quilted hands reaching upwards. The whole represents Oxfam's relentless struggle for a fairer world. Car spray painted and hand quilted.

28 x 55 in (71 x 140 cm)

Children's Circle
Jennie Loudon, Edinburgh, Scotland

A wallhanging to represent the fact that children around the world all have status and equal importance. Drawn by Emily in a 'Georgetown Circle' framework of recycled silk scraps on a cotton background. Machine appliqué and embroidery, machine and hand quilted.

32 x 32 in (81 x 81 cm)

Flowers All Around the World
K. Philp (88 years old), Benfleet, Essex

The quilt consists of a symbolic world surrounded by flowers in yellows, oranges, creams and browns. The maker hopes that it will contribute to a fairer world in both senses of the word. Hand pieced over papers.

88 x 90 in (224 x 229 cm)

Fabric of Oxfam
Gill Turley, Dorking, Surrey

Grey, blue, cream and rust coloured shirts from Oxfam shops make up the fabric of this quilt. By cutting, pinning, piecing, tacking and quilting the fabrics something new is created out of something old mirroring the work of Oxfam's shops. In keeping with the rustic look of the quilt, the layers are secured with 'Mennonite Tacks' and a small amount of hand quilting has been worked in the centre.

54 x 76 in (137 x 193 cm)

Niñez Campesina (Peasant Children)
Allpa, Jesus Maria, Peru (via Oxfam Trading)

A hand-painted quilt on a melon coloured background. The picture shows a group of children looking for new horizons. Machine stitched.

28 x 45 in (72 x 114 cm)

The Flower Patch
Hadleigh Woodfield Townswomen's Guild,
Benfleet, Essex

Hexagon flowers in pinks and blues set into a
plain pink background present an image of
Oxfam's fairer world. Hand pieced over papers.

83 x 90 in (211 x 229 cm)

Niña Jugando (Child Playing)
Allpa, Jesus Maria, Peru (via Oxfam Trading)

The quilt is made from remnants of cloth and
wool. It shows a young girl playing with a 3D doll
in traditional Peruvian dress. Machine and hand
sewn appliqué, machine assembled.

27 x 37 in (69 x 95 cm)

**The following quilts were all obtained via
Oxfam Trading and submitted to the general part of the QUILTS U.K. exhibition.**

Mela

Narayanganj Group, Kumudini, Bangladesh (via
Oxfam Trading)

This panel is a collection of scenes from Bengali folklore arranged vertically in sections. One tale is of a tiger hunt, another shows the Moyur Ponkhi or luxurious, peacock-shaped boats of the past. There is the picture of a ferry boat crossing a river, a snake dancing in response to a snake charmer and a servant tending her wealthy master with a fan and hubble bubble. All around are bunches of flowers and roughly-sketched animals producing an impression of restlessness - of moving from one scene to another, one emotion to another - all balanced by a steady pride in the ancient tradition of which this Nakshi Kantha work (see page 16) is a part. Hand stitched.

22 x 37 in (55 x 94 cm)

Phuler Jagat (World Flowers)

Bachte Shekha Group, Jessore, Bangladesh

This is a copy of a traditional Nakshi Kantha quilt (see page 16) in Dhaka Museum, stitched by the Bachte Shekha group, whose name means 'learning to become self reliant'. In the centre of the quilt is a lotus flower representing life. This is surrounded by other flower motifs and rich animals, such as the elephant and the horse. Hand stitched.

102 x 100 in (259 x 254 cm)

Palki-Bou (Bride in Palanquin)
Kushtia Group, Kumudini, Bangladesh

A copy of a traditional Nakshi Kantha museum piece (see page 16). The central motif is of a bride gazing out of a palanquin. The journey signifies a transition from one phase of life to another. The two are linked, but we can never go back. As we go forward there will be echoes of forgotten lifetimes. The scenes surrounding the bride could be from her childhood or from her life to come, giving a timeless quality to the quilt. Hand stitched.

86 x 36 in (218 x 91 cm)

Detail of the central motif (above)

Child's Hanging
Narayanganj Group, Kumudini, Bangladesh (via Oxfam Trading)

This red wallhanging was made by a group of Bangladeshi women and designed for a children's room. It shows the animals who are admired as the King of the Beasts. Hope for a bright and prosperous future is expressed in the use of colours. Hope for their children's success is contained in the choice of royal animals. The work is traditional Nakshi Kantha quilting (see page 16). Hand stitched.

37 x 29 in (94 x 74 cm)

Amar Swapna (My Hope and Dream)

Narayanganj Group, Kumudini, Bangladesh (via Oxfam Trading)

This traditional red Nakshi Kantha quilt is a typical example of this intricate style of stitching (see page 16). The Kantha is full of animals in pairs and birds flying with twigs in their beaks ready to build their nests. Bright colours express hope and happiness, while the boats and elephants represent a prosperous future. Hand stitched.

30 x 39 in (76 x 99 cm)

Digbaj (Somersault)

Bogra Group, Kumudini, Bangladesh

A patchwork quilt made up of eighteen Nakshi Kantha blocks (see page 16), joined by sashing strips, and full of happy, rather mad images. There are animals, children performing impossible somersaults and what could be parrots walking round in a circle. The whole scene is perhaps just a village maiden's idea of an imaginary circus, such as she has heard tell of but never seen. Hand stitched.

63 x 103 in (160 x 262 cm)

About Quilts U.K.

In just three years Quilts U.K. has become the annual quilt show not to be missed. Visitors travel by coach and car from all over Britain and many come from overseas - the U.S.A., Australia, New Zealand and Europe. Entries for the show are also worldwide.

In 1992 over 500 quilts and wallhanging were submitted - a record so far. There is always a wide variety of quilting and other craft stalls, demonstrations and a food hall: car parking is free.

The Severn Hall and adjacent marquee allow the quilts to be displayed to advantage whether king-size or miniature. The bed quilts tend to be traditional in design and subdued in colour to become lasting treasures in the home, while the wallhangings can have a more dramatic impact for home, office or public display. What today's patchworkers and quilters can achieve with fabrics, needle and thread has to be seen to be believed.

The three judges for 1992 are Jean Eitel, editor of several American quilting magazines, Dorothy Osler, an authority on British quilts with several books to her credit and Gillian Clarke, a well-known English quiltmaker and tireless worker for the charity Oxfam. Further information about the judges appears on the next page.

Quilts U.K. were delighted to help Oxfam celebrate its 50th Anniversary Year by offering a special theme category; 'Oxfam - 50 Years Working for a Fairer World'. The time spent making the quilts for this category has been totalled to give a grand contribution of over 3,000 days to Oxfam's 'Million Day Appeal'.

Mrs Amy Emms, made an M.B.E. for her services to quilting, travelled down from her home in Cumbria to present the prizes. Although in her eighties, Mrs Emms delights in meeting quilters, demonstrating her skills and seeing how the craft she helped to keep alive in the 1930s blossomed in the 1990s.

Quilts U.K. is organized by Mrs Elaine Hammond and Mrs Dianne Huck, both avid quilters. They also produce 'Patchwork & Quilting', a quarterly magazine whose aim is to promote the crafts of patchwork and quilting by sustaining and creating interest through the exchange of ideas and information.

Each issue contains clearly explained projects for both beginners and the more experienced, and is packed with features and news and views of the quilting world to provide even more inspiration. The attractive and informative layout of the magazine provides a solid and valuable source of reference for anyone who is interested in these crafts.

Since its inception in 1985, the number of pages in 'Patchwork & Quilting', has been increased. Many are now in full colour. Circulation has also increased and the readership is worldwide.

For further information concerning Quilts U.K. and 'Patchwork & Quilting' contact:
Mrs Elaine Hammond or Mrs Dianne Huck, Quilts U.K., Ingsdon, 1 Highfield Close, Malvern Link, Worcestershire WR14 1SH

About the Judges

JEAN EITEL

Jean is a native of Palm Beach, Florida, US.A. and is an Editor of several quilting magazines published by Harris Publication, New York.

Following a college education in Fine Arts and Textiles, Jean has always worked in the needlecraft industry. She has judged several of the major quilt festivals in the United States and Europe. She teaches patchwork and quilting at national and international seminars, and has written a book: 'Creative Quiltmaking in the Mandala Tradition' published by Chilton Books.

Here are Jean's thoughts on quilting:
'Quiltmaking, lecturing, writing and teaching quilting have been primary activities in my life for the last decade. These activities are the result of an educational background in fine arts and a lifelong involvement in the needlearts. I believe that making a quilt is an artistic journey in which the process of working out the design, colour, symbolism and textural components of each piece is as important as the finished product.

I learn something new about myself and my abilities as an artist as I embark on each new quiltmaking adventure.'

DOROTHY OSLER

Dorothy Osler has channelled a lifelong interest in textile crafts into being a quilter, writer and teacher. She travels widely, giving classes on quilting throughout Britain as well as in Europe and the U.S.A. She combines practical skills with an unrivalled academic knowledge of the history and social traditions of British quilting, for which she is internationally known.

Over the past 20 years, her activities within the growing world of patchwork and quilting have also included: serving for six years as the first Heritage Officer of the Quilters' Guild: judging at both national and international exhibitions; currently acting as both tutor and verifier for the City & Guilds Patchwork & Quilting Course; and writing three books, the most recent of which 'Quilting' - was published in 1991 by Merehurst-Fairfax.

GILLIAN CLARKE

Gillian Clarke has been a lifelong stitcher, and particularly enjoys quiltmaking. Her original and well-executed designs have won prizes, and have brought pleasure to their owners. The wedding quilt she made for her daughter was shown at Quilts U.K. 1992. Gillian is also an active campaigner for Oxfam and has contributed the introduction to this book.

THE QUILTERS

Maxine Addison, Whickham, Newcastle-on-Tyne
Margot Agnew, Chorley, Lancashire
Allpa, Jesus Maria, Peru
Sheila Arthurs, Castle Vale, Birmingham
Avonbourne School Quilters, Bournemouth
Bachte Shekha, Bangladesh
Rita Ball, Callington, Cornwall
Sue Barry, Loughborough, Leicestershire
Sue Barry, Jenni Dobson, Mary Logan,
    Loughborough, Leicestershire
Berkhamsted Quilters, Bovingdon, Hertfordshire
Dawn Berry, Cheltenham, Gloucestershire
Yvonne Blatchford, Shirley, Southampton,
    Hampshire
Bogra Group, Kumudini, Bangladesh
Borderers Quilting Group, Ludlow, Shropshire
Bothwell Quilters Glasgow
Boxgrove & Merrow Townswomen's Guild,
    Guildford, Surrey
BRAC, Bangladesh
Hilda Bradbury, Bridgenorth, Shropshire
Bristol Quilters Afternoon Group, Bristol
Diana Brockway, Newport, Gwent
Maureen Cassells, Renfrew, Scotland
Catherine Infant School Friday Sewing Group,
    Leicester
Year 8, Chauncy School, Ware, Hertfordshire
Averil Clavey, Cockermouth, Cumbria
Janet Cook, Felmersham, Bedford
Lynne Cooke, Malvern, Worcestershire
Danetre Quilters, Northampton
Didcot Townswomen's Guild, Didcot, Oxfordshire
Jean England, Pury End, Northamptonshire
Maureen Evans Southampton, Hampshire
Bernadette Falvey, Barna, Galway, Eire
Fedanp, Colombia
Four Oaks First School, Sutton Coldfield, West
    Midlands
Goblin Coombe Quilters, Cleeve, Avon
Sarah Greenwood, London
Rosemary Gregory, Wolverhampton,
    Staffordshire
Grupo Asociativo Los Andes, Colombia
Hadleigh Woodfield Townswomen's Guild,
    Benfleet, Essex
Mary Hewson, New Milton, Hampshire
Susan Hill, Wrexham, Clwyd
Hitchin Oxfam Shop, Hitchin, Hertfordshire
Rita Hodges, Berkhamsted, Hertfordshire
Avril Hopcraft, Milton Keynes, Buckinghamshire
Maureen Hoyle, Lymm, Cheshire
Margaret Hughes, Anglesey, Gwynedd
Ilford Oxfam Group, Ilford, Essex
Pam Ironmonger, Brixham, Devon
Pauline Jackson, Broughton-in-Furness, Cumbria
Philippa Johnston, Sutton, Surrey
Pam Keeling, Barton Seagrave, Kettering,
    Northamptonshire
Kendal Oxfam Group, Kendal, Cumbria
Kushtia Group, Kumudini, Bangladesh
Avril Lansdell, Kingston-upon-Thames, Surrey
Launceston Oxfam Helpers, Cornwall
Launton Ladies Sewing Circle, Bicester,
    Oxfordshire
Pam Le Bas, Leicester
Freda Lee, Windermere, Cumbria
Lleyn Delyn Quilters, Mold, Clwyd
Jennie Loudon, Edinburgh
Yvonne Loudon, Portishead, Bristol
Catherine MacLeod, Frodsham, Cheshire
Mary Mayne, Dunstable, Bedfordshire
Irene Maxwell, Sidcup, Kent
Measham Quilters, Swadlincote, Derbyshire

Jenny Morgan, Llandrindod Wells, Powys
Kathy Morton, Sutton-in-Ashfield, Nottinghamshire
Geraldine Mundy, Milton Keynes,
    Buckinghamshire
Narayanganj Group, Kumudini, Bangladesh
Dorothy Organ, Epping, Essex
Orleton School, Orleton, Ludlow, Shropshire
Oxfam Shop Group, Newcastle, Staffordshire
Joanne Pate, Keighley, Yorkshire
Peartree Quilters, St. Albans, Hertfordshire
K Philp, Benfleet, Essex
Portishead Quilters, Portishead, Bristol
Angela Raby, Northfield, Birmingham
Raya Quilters, Tavistock, Devon
Norine Redman, Milton Keynes, Buckinghamshire
Dora Ryder, Kidderminster, Worcestershire
Sabina Co-op, Ahmedabad, India
Constance Sara, Stroud, Gloucestershire
Sheila Scawen, Bradwell, Sheffield
J. Scothern, Mapperley, Nottingham
Seva Sangh Samity & Self-help Handicrafts
    Society, co-ordinated by Sasha, Calcutta, India
Seva Sangh Samity & Panchannagram Mahila
    Samity, co-ordinated by Sasha, Calcutta, India
Elizabeth Skinner, West Haddon,
    Northamptonshire
Mary Slade, Kings Norton, Birmingham
Margaret Smith, Shipton Oliffe, Cheltenham,
    Gloucestershire
Rosemary Southam, Chalfont St. Peter,
    Buckinghamshire
Mary Stevens, Southam, Warwickshire
Anne-Marie Stewart, Ipswich, Suffolk
Surrey Young Quilters, Dorking, Surrey
Taller Libertad, Colombia
K Tombs, Cobham, Surrey
Totternhoe Quilters, Dunstable, Bedfordshire
Gill Turley, Dorking, Surrey
Maggie Ward, Grandpont, Oxford
Tric Watkins, Trescott, Wolverhampton
Aeileish Watts, Worcester
Hannah Watts, Worcester
Jane Wheat, Radcliffe-on-Trent, Nottingham
Catherine Williams, Bishop's Stortford
Jane Williams, Wolverhampton, Staffordshire
Kate Williams, Wolverhampton, Staffordshire
Kiran Williams Wolverhampton, Staffordshire
Sylvia Williams, Llandrindod Wells, Powys
White Wells Quilters, Ilkley, West Yorkshire
Beverley Wood, Winchester, Hampshire
Rosie Wood, Eastbourne, East Sussex
YWCA Dhaka, Bangladesh

The following have donated their quilts to Oxfam:

Maxine Addison
Margot Agnew
Sheila Arthurs
Avonbourne School Quilters
Sue Barry
Sue Barry, Jenni Dobson and Mary Logan
Berkhamsted Quilters
Yvonne Blatchford
Borderers Quilting Group
Bothwell Quilters
Joan A Bowie
Boxgrove & Merrow Townswomen's Guild
Bristol Quilters Afternoon Group
Catherine Infant School Friday Sewing Group

Averil Clavey
Janet Cook
Lynne Cooke
Danetre Quilters
Didcot Townswomen's Guild
Jean England
Maureen Evans
Bernadette Falvey
Four Oaks First School
Goblin Coombe Quilters
Trisha J Goodwin
Rosemary Gregory
Hadleigh Woodfield Townswomen's Guild
Mary Hewson
Susan Hill
Hitchin Oxfam Shop
Avril Hopcraft
Maureen Hoyle
Margaret Hughes
Ilford Oxfam Group
Pam Ironmonger
Philippa Johnston
Avril Lansdell
Launceston Oxfam Helpers
Launton Ladies Sewing Circle
Freda Lee
Lleyn Delyn Quilters
Jennie Loudon
Yvonne Loudon
Mary Mayne
Irene Maxwell
Measham Quilters
Jenny Morgan
Kathy Morton
Geraldine Mundy
Dorothy Organ
Orleton School
Oxfam Shop Group
Joanne Pate
D V Patrick
Peartree Quilters
K Philp
Portishead Quilters
Angela Raby
Raya Quilters
Norine Redman
Sheila Scawen
J. Scothern
Elizabeth Skinner
Mary Slade
Rosemary Southam
Mary Stevens
K Tombs
Totternhoe Quilters
Maggie Ward
Tric Watkins
Aeileish Watts
Rebecca Weeks
Catherine Williams
Jane Williams
Sylvia Williams
White Wells Quilters
Beverley Wood
Rosie Wood

On 5 October, 1942, a group of people formed the Oxford Committee for Famine Relief. Its aim was to relieve the sufferings of civilians in Greece and to press for supplies to be allowed through the Allied blockade. In 1965 the charity adopted its telegram name, Oxfam.

Oxfam now works in seventy-seven countries and supports nearly 3,000 long-term development projects. Much of its work is in places where conflict makes life almost unsupportable for innocent victims. A common theme through Oxfam's development is the commitment to humanitarian help for people, irrespective of religious or political boundaries.

Oxfam still carries out emergency work but is also committed to the more lasting relief of suffering. It works alongside the very poorest people, supporting them in their efforts to break free of sickness, illiteracy, powerlessness and poverty. Through this work it helps to challenge the exploitation and injustice that keeps people poor.

Many self-help projects are small scale, needing minimal financial support. About a third of Oxfam grants are for under £3,000, but the impact of these small sums is considerable. After decades of experience, Oxfam knows that the projects most likely to succeed are those in which people are working for their own development.

Working for a Fairer World

Oxfam's support comes in many ways:

• an improvement in life for the woman who can draw water from a new well without having to walk many kilometres.

• shelter and support for a refugee, even for a short time.

• two meals a day, instead of one, as a result of improved agricultural methods.

• a landless farmer getting title to land, and with it the freedom to feed his family.

• relief given by someone who is prepared to listen to your troubles.

• the joy of a mother whose child's life has been saved by oral rehydration.

• the lifting of some oppression through the activity of an unknown friend in a far country, who cared enough to write to his or her M.P.

Oxfam gives an opportunity for everyone to make this support possible, to make our world a fairer place. By buying this book you have already contributed, through the royalty Oxfam will receive.

There are other ways you can work with Oxfam for a fairer world. You could:

• give good quality books, toys, clothes or other things you no longer need to an Oxfam shop.

• save stamps or coins and drop them off at an Oxfam shop.

• talk to other people about ways of working for a fairer world and get yourself and them involved.

• volunteer your time and your skills to work with Oxfam - in a shop, as a compaigner, as a speaker, as a house-to-house collector, as a fund raiser.

• introduce Oxfam to organizations to which you belong - to church groups, social clubs, playgroups, trades unions, professional bodies, sports clubs.

Oxfam Projects

Here are just a few of the thousands of projects that Oxfam has supported:

BOLIVIA Centro de Promoción de la Mujer: salaries, materials, transport and childcare costs for women's project.

INDONESIA Yayasan Swakarsa: funds to buy cows for income generation with poor transmigrants in Bengkulu.

MOZAMBIQUE Ex-Infantario: provision of two sewing machines for group of trained tailors and their apprentices living in remote centre for disabled veterans and civilians.

PAKISTAN Presentation Convent Sargodha: support for screen-printing workshops for women.

PERU Comite de Pequeñas Empresas y Micro-Empresas de Limitados (CODEL): food, equipment, medicines and orthopaedic aids for rehabilitation of people with disabilities in shanty areas.

UGANDA Ankole Women Self-Help Association (AWSHA): bicycles, hoes, gunny bags, weeding and tractor hire.

To find out more about Oxfam, contact us in:

ENGLAND: Oxfam Anniversary Information, 274 Banbury Road, Oxford OX2 7DZ

IRELAND: Oxfam, 202 Lower Rathmines Road, Dublin 6

NORTHERN IRELAND: Oxfam, P.O.Box 70, 52-54 Dublin Road, Belfast BT2 7HN

SCOTLAND: Oxfam, 5th floor, Fleming House, 134 Renfrew Street, Glasgow G3 3T

WALES: Oxfam, 46-48 Station Road, Llanishen, Cardiff CF4 5LU

AUSTRALIA: Community Aid Abroad, 156 George Street, Fitzroy, Victoria 3065

BELGIUM Oxfam Belgique, 39 rue du Conseil, 1050 Brussels

CANADA Oxfam Canada, 251 Laurier Avenue West, Room 301, Ottawa, Ontario K1P 5J6

HONG KONG Oxfam, Ground Floor-3B, June Garden, 28 Tung Chau Street, Tai Kok Tsui, Kowloon

NEW ZEALAND Oxfam New Zealand, Room 101 La Gonda House, 203 Karangahape Road, Auckland 1

QUEBEC Oxfam Quebec, 169 rue St Paul est, Montreal 127, Quebec H2Y 1G8

U.S.A. Oxfam America, 115 Broadway, Boston, Massachusetts 02116